TRUE YOU

A SELF-DISCOVERY JOURNAL

OF PROMPTS & EXERCISES TO INSPIRE REFLECTION & GROWTH

Kelly Vincent, PsyD

Illustrations by Jacinta Kay

ROCKRIDGE
PRESS

Interior and Cover Designer: Linda Snorina

Photo Art Director/Art Manager: Tom Hood

Editor: Lori Tenny

Production Editor: Ashley Polikoff

Illustrations © Jacinta Kay, 2020

Author Photo © Amber Thrane

Illustrator Photo © Grace Petrou

ISBN: 978-1-64611-633-1

R0

To you,

for having the courage and curiosity

to explore who you are.

CONTENTS

"The most adventurous journey

to embark on is the journey to yourself;

the most exciting thing to discover is

who you really are; the most treasured pieces

that you can find are all the pieces of you;

the most special portrait you can recognize

is the portrait of your soul."

—C. Joybell C.

INTRODUCTION

I am so glad you are here. It takes a lot of courage, bravery, and strength to allow space for yourself to dig deep and discover who you are, what you love, and what you desire out of life.

My name is Dr. Kelly Vincent, and I am a licensed psychologist who is passionate about helping, empowering, and supporting women. Through my personal journey, coupled with my clinical work, I have experienced and witnessed the power of self-discovery. When we look inward, and I mean *really* look, we find and understand things about ourselves that we may have never recognized, contemplated, or understood before. This can be so impactful in the way we live, how we are with others, and how we view the world.

This journal is an invitation and guide for you to begin your self-exploration. The activities and exercises were thoughtfully crafted to inspire you to peel back the layers and uncover the essence of who you truly are.

So why journal, anyway? It is probably safe to say you are interested in self-discovery. You wouldn't be holding this journal if you weren't. The journey of self-discovery is a fluid process in which we are constantly growing, evolving, and changing. Becoming deeply acquainted with yourself can serve as an extremely therapeutic experience, as it provides you the space to feel, process, and release emotions. Research shows journaling can help clarify thoughts and feelings, reduce stress, solve problems more effectively, resolve disagreements with others, and allow space for more creativity to flow, according to a Psych Central article by Maud Purcell.

When we stop and take the time to really understand ourselves, we begin to cultivate the most important relationship of our lives—the relationship with ourselves. Don't get me wrong; dedicating time and space for this process can be very challenging. As you venture along, raw and uncomfortable feelings may surface. Just know that this is perfectly normal—and, if you ask me, a good thing! We want to acknowledge, validate, and, most importantly, experience those feelings. On the flip side, engaging in this process can ignite insight, understanding, contentment, satisfaction, and peace within ourselves. Who doesn't need a little peace in their life?

How to Use This Journal

The intention of this journal is to provide space to process and develop a holistic understanding of yourself, while also giving you actionable tools to integrate into your life. It is composed of various exercises and prompts within several specific topical sections that will inspire you to explore in a variety of meaningful ways. This journal is organized in a way that addresses the important aspects of self-discovery, which often starts with self-awareness, while also defining your values, passions, identity, confidence, goals, dreams, and life purpose. There is also space to further explore your family dynamics, mind, emotions, relationships, spirituality, health, career, finances, and community. I encourage you to use the journal in whatever way serves you. Perhaps you want to dedicate time each day or set aside "me time" once per week. Know that this is your process and finding a cadence that works is the most important thing. Some of the prompts may be extra thought-provoking, so don't forget that you can always start an exercise and come back to it later when you feel ready.

At the end of the day, meeting ourselves for the first time can be scary. However, it can help us recognize the amazingness we have within. I am inviting you to step onto your path of self-discovery and uncover your perfectly imperfect self with the intention of finding clarity, insight, and feelings of empowerment, inspiration, and growth. Remember, you are the only version of yourself that exists. Being your authentic self is one of the best gifts you can give yourself.

Are you ready to meet the true you? I believe you are. Your journey begins here. Let's dive in!

SELF-AWARENESS

"I'm very interested in truth,

in finding ways to be messy

and unsure and flawed and incredible

and great and my fullest self,

all wrapped into one."

—Emma Watson

Our friends and family often see us differently than we see ourselves. If you wrote an autobiography, what story would you tell? How would you describe your characteristics and distinguishing qualities?

Now, what if your sibling or best friend wrote a biography about you? What would they say?

With an open heart and honest mind, you can unlock the deeper layers of yourself. Find a quiet space, get cozy, and let it flow.

I believe...

My biggest fear is...

I get frustrated when...

I am happiest when…

My hope for myself is…

My biggest regret is…

I feel authentic when…

Social media is powerful. It can connect us in wonderful ways, but it can also provoke mindless scrolling, overanalysis of captions, and a need to edit and filter our life. How do you present yourself on social media? What parts of your life do you share? What parts do you hide and why? Can you be more authentically you?

Becoming more aware of joyful moments and experiences of gratitude and daily learning can boost our mood, build insight, and decrease stress. As you move through your day, take notice of the things that ignite joy, gratitude, and knowledge.

Today, I felt joy when...

Today, I'm grateful for...

Today, I learned...

VALUES

"I HAVE LEARNED THAT AS LONG AS I HOLD FAST TO MY BELIEFS AND VALUES——AND FOLLOW MY OWN MORAL COMPASS——THEN THE ONLY EXPECTATIONS I NEED TO LIVE UP TO ARE MY OWN."

—Michelle Obama

Think of a person who you really admire. Why do you value or respect this person? What aspect of their value system resonates with you? How can you apply similar attributes or values to your life?

Values are foundational principles and a reflection of our true selves. They are often passed down from our family or evolve from life experiences. What values resonate with you? What is important to you? Write about any and all that come to mind, using those mentioned on the right as inspiration.

AUTHENTICITY freedom
COMPASSION INTEGRITY
honesty KINDNESS STATUS
recognition WORK ETHIC
BRAVERY SPIRITUALITY love
relationships KNOWLEDGE
generosity GROWTH OPTIMISM
perseverance wealth loyalty
RESPECT creativity
FAMILY security
EQUALITY ENTREPRENEURSHIP
SUCCESS STABILITY CURIOSITY

Values can serve as our guide, helping us navigate life and its challenges. Using your list on the previous page, let's narrow down and explore your core values. For each of the eight points on the compass, name a core value. On the next page, write about why these are important to you.

When our actions align with our values, we begin to live more authentically. Developing an action associated with our values can create feelings of fulfillment and joy. For each of your eight core values, write one action (or more) that you can associate with that value. It can be a daily, weekly, or monthly action.

EXAMPLE:

CORE VALUE: *Connection*

ACTION: *Plan monthly social dates, call parents and/or extended family weekly*

CORE VALUE:

ACTION:

CORE VALUE:

ACTION:

CORE VALUE:

ACTION:

CORE VALUE:

ACTION:

CORE VALUE:

ACTION:

CORE VALUE:

ACTION:

CORE VALUE:

ACTION:

CORE VALUE:

ACTION:

CORE VALUE:

ACTION:

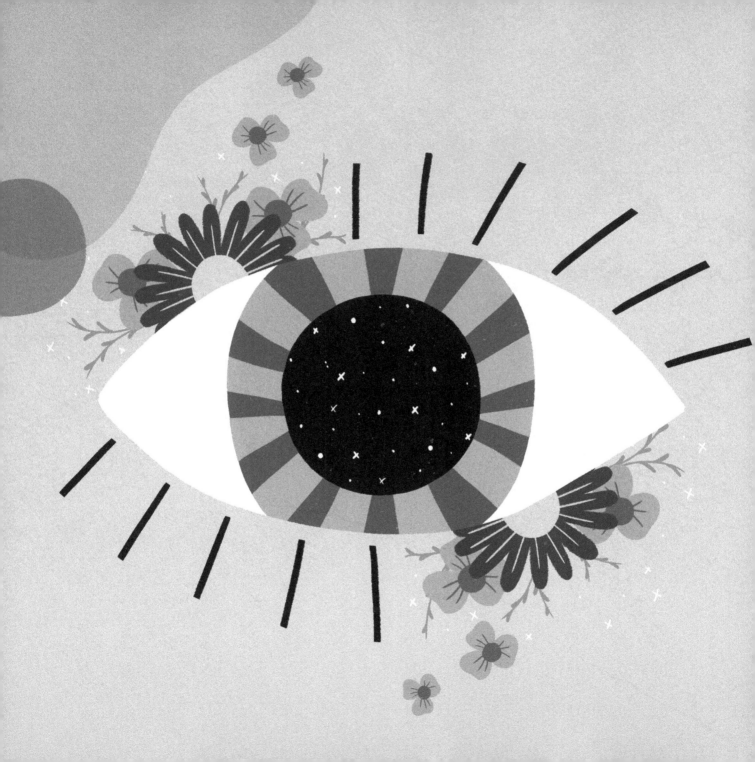

IDENTITY

"ONE OF THE MOST COURAGEOUS THINGS YOU CAN DO
IS IDENTIFY YOURSELF, KNOW WHO YOU ARE,
WHAT YOU BELIEVE IN, AND WHERE YOU WANT TO GO."

—Sheila Murray Bethel

Identity can be described as our core and authentic self. Identity attributes often include gender, age, race, ethnicity, personality characteristics, and cultural descriptions. How do you identify? Write about any and all identities that resonate with you.

I am...

Beliefs about ourselves are often rooted in our life experiences and can sometimes be intertwined with our identity. They can be empowering (e.g., "I am lovable") or disempowering (e.g., "I am not good enough"). What experiences in your life have created beliefs about yourself?

EXAMPLES:

EXPERIENCE: *My mom was hyper-focused on weight.*
BELIEF: *If I am skinny, I am beautiful.*

EXPERIENCE: *Effort was often praised in my family.*
BELIEF: *I am capable if I put my mind to it.*

EXPERIENCE:

BELIEF:

EXPERIENCE:

BELIEF:

EXPERIENCE:

BELIEF:

EXPERIENCE:

BELIEF:

EXPERIENCE:

BELIEF:

EXPERIENCE:

BELIEF:

EXPERIENCE:

BELIEF:

EXPERIENCE:

BELIEF:

EXPERIENCE:

BELIEF:

Pick three limiting beliefs from the previous exercise. Are these beliefs accurate? Do you have evidence to support them? How could you challenge these limiting beliefs? What would it feel like to know these beliefs are not true?

Mantras are often single words or simple phrases that have the power to alter how we see ourselves. They can be helpful when challenging limiting beliefs. Write down a few mantras (e.g., "I am enough"). Recite them aloud for three minutes, maybe in front of a mirror. Describe your experience.

CONFIDENCE

"THE MOST BEAUTIFUL THING YOU CAN WEAR IS CONFIDENCE."

—Blake Lively

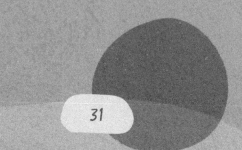

Think of a time when you were able to overcome a difficult situation. Describe the situation. What strengths within yourself did you use to get through it? What did you learn about life and yourself after the situation?

Celebrating and recognizing ourselves is one of the keys to feeling confident. Whether big or small, we do great things each day that often go unrecognized. Make a list of your strengths (e.g., ambition), personality attributes (e.g., honesty), and proud moments (e.g., getting promoted).

STRENGTHS:

PERSONALITY ATTRIBUTES:

PROUD MOMENTS:

The way we think and talk about our body is a big contributor to our overall confidence. We are often at odds with our body, instead of embracing and loving it. Write a love letter to your body. What do you appreciate about it? What do you love or feel grateful for?

Dear Body,

Love,

We all battle that pesky voice within that can bombard us with unhelpful thoughts about ourselves and others. In order to minimize this inner critic, we first must become aware of it and then challenge it. Make a list of your typical inner critic thoughts. Then elaborate on how your inner bestie would challenge those thoughts.

MIND

"YOU MUST LEARN A NEW WAY TO THINK BEFORE YOU CAN MASTER A NEW WAY TO BE."

—Marianne Williamson

Thoughts are not facts. When we look at negative thoughts through a more realistic lens, we have the power to alter our mood and outlook on life. Let's decode our thoughts using an exercise based on the principles of cognitive behavioral therapy. What's triggered you recently? Follow the prompts.

EXAMPLE:

ACTIVATING EXPERIENCE: *My partner broke up with me.*

BELIEF/THOUGHT: *I am unlovable. People always break up with me. What is wrong with me?*

EMOTIONAL AND BEHAVIORAL CONSEQUENCE: *I am depressed and isolating myself.*

DISPUTING THE NEGATIVE THOUGHT/BELIEF: *I have so much to offer, I am enough, and I deserve to be loved. This was not the right relationship for me.*

ACTIVATING EXPERIENCE:

BELIEF/THOUGHT:

EMOTIONAL AND BEHAVIORAL CONSEQUENCE:

DISPUTING THE NEGATIVE THOUGHT/BELIEF:

ACTIVATING EXPERIENCE:

BELIEF/THOUGHT:

EMOTIONAL AND BEHAVIORAL CONSEQUENCE:

DISPUTING THE NEGATIVE THOUGHT/BELIEF:

ACTIVATING EXPERIENCE:

BELIEF/THOUGHT:

EMOTIONAL AND BEHAVIORAL CONSEQUENCE:

DISPUTING THE NEGATIVE THOUGHT/BELIEF:

Our mind often clings to past experiences that left us feeling hurt, in pain, or sad. Think of a few of those experiences and note them in the balloons below.

Now, close your eyes and visualize each experience as a balloon. When you are ready, let go of each balloon and watch it float into the sky. What thoughts, feelings, and sensations came up as you let go?

When we are feeling depressed, our minds are often in the past, and when we are feeling anxious, our minds are often in the future. If we shift and focus more on the present, we often can find a sense of peace and relief. Think about a time when you were fully present. Describe it. Where were you? What were you doing? What thoughts, feelings, and sensations did you notice?

Visualization is a superfood for the mind and a powerful tool. Draw or describe in detail a dream you have for yourself.

Now, close your eyes and visualize the dream as if it has already come true. What does it feel like? How is your life different? What is it like to have achieved this dream?

EMOTIONS

"The best and most beautiful things in the world cannot be seen or even touched.

They must be felt with the heart."

—Helen Keller

Emotional awareness and expression are often modeled to us by our caregivers. Think back to your childhood. How were emotions expressed in your home? What emotions were more commonly expressed (e.g., joy)? What emotions were avoided (e.g., sadness)?

Becoming aware of your emotions is a powerful skill. What emotion do you find difficult to control (e.g., anxiety)? Draw the emotion.

If you had to give the emotion a name, what would you name it (e.g., Miss Fire)? What sensations do you notice when you feel it? In what situations does it come up? Where do you think it might be rooted?

Learning how to acknowledge and communicate our feelings can have a profound effect on our overall well-being. When we learn how to recognize and express our feelings in a direct, assertive, and concise way, we often feel heard, seen, and validated. Let's practice.

I feel...

because...

I notice strong feelings often arise in my body, particularly my...

When I am feeling emotional, I tend to...

This week, I am feeling...

What I need more of is...

_____ makes me feel...

Think of an emotion you would like to let go of (e.g., resentment) and an emotion you want more of (e.g., peace). Write them below.

I am letting go of...

I am inviting more _____ into my life.

Now, close your eyes. On your next inhale, breathe in the emotion you want more of, and on your exhale, breathe out the emotion you are letting go of. Repeat for a few rounds as you slowly breathe in and out. What was this experience like?

SPIRITUALITY

"SPIRITUALITY IS RECOGNIZING AND CELEBRATING THAT WE ARE ALL INEXTRICABLY CONNECTED TO EACH OTHER BY A POWER GREATER THAN ALL OF US, AND THAT OUR CONNECTION TO THAT POWER AND TO ONE ANOTHER IS GROUNDED IN LOVE AND COMPASSION. PRACTICING SPIRITUALITY BRINGS A SENSE OF PERSPECTIVE, MEANING, AND PURPOSE TO OUR LIVES."

—Brené Brown

Spirituality can look different for each person. It may include a connection with nature or a higher power of some sort. How would you define your spirituality? What does it look like for you? What does it feel like?

Some define spirituality as a connection back to the greater good or the universe. What do you believe makes the world a better place? More importantly, how can you positively impact the world?

Spirituality can sometimes encourage us to find a deeper meaning in life. When you think about your life today, what gives you meaning? Name and describe the people, places, and things that provide meaning.

Spiritual practices can help us cultivate genuine authenticity and a connection to ourselves. Some practices may be done daily, such as meditation, prayer, spending time alone, or self-exploration. What are some spiritual practices you would like to regularly engage in and why?

HEALTH

"Caring for your own body, mind, and spirit is your greatest (and grandest) responsibility. It's about listening to the needs of your soul and then honoring them."

—Kristi Ling

We live in a world where we are constantly flooded with messages about how to be healthy, from the foods we should be eating to what workouts to try to how to look and feel younger. The real question is, what does healthy mean to you? In the illustration below, note what areas of health are most important to you (e.g., exercise, mental health, clean eating, etc.).

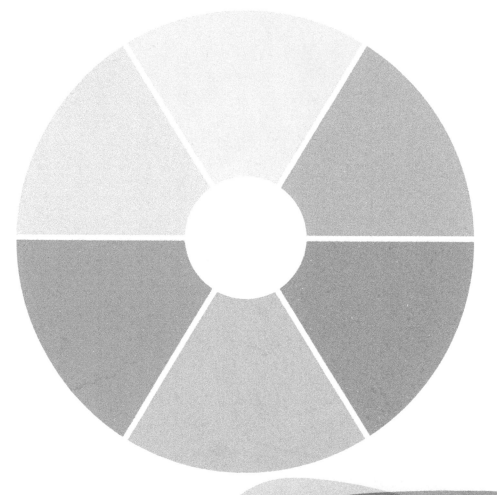

Now, elaborate on why these healthy behaviors are important to you.

Sometimes we become consumed with thoughts about how to be healthier. If you were given a magic wand that could make you perfectly healthy, what would that look like to you? What often gets in the way of achieving your health goals? What are some ideas for overcoming the challenges?

EXAMPLE:

HEALTH IDEAL: *Looking toned and fit*

WHAT GETS IN MY WAY: *Work, stress, obligations*

WAYS TO OVERCOME THE CHALLENGES: *Schedule exercise into routine*

HEALTH IDEAL:

WHAT GETS IN MY WAY:

WAYS TO OVERCOME THE CHALLENGES:

HEALTH IDEAL:

WHAT GETS IN MY WAY:

WAYS TO OVERCOME THE CHALLENGES:

HEALTH IDEAL:

WHAT GETS IN MY WAY:

WAYS TO OVERCOME THE CHALLENGES:

HEALTH IDEAL:

WHAT GETS IN MY WAY:

WAYS TO OVERCOME THE CHALLENGES:

HEALTH IDEAL:

WHAT GETS IN MY WAY:

WAYS TO OVERCOME THE CHALLENGES:

HEALTH IDEAL:

WHAT GETS IN MY WAY:

WAYS TO OVERCOME THE CHALLENGES:

Being consistently healthy is not a solo endeavor. It sometimes takes support from friends, family, and professionals. If you could form a "health team," who could you recruit? Write their names below. Could one of those individuals serve as your accountability coach as you work toward your goals? In what ways could they help support you?

It can be difficult to be healthy 100 percent of the time. We are human, after all. However, it can be helpful to plan health-related goals each week. What health-related activities (e.g., meal planning, exercise, meditation) would you like to engage in this week?

SUNDAY:

MONDAY:

TUESDAY:

WEDNESDAY:

THURSDAY:

FRIDAY:

SATURDAY:

FAMILY

"Call it a clan, call it a network,
call it a tribe, call it a family.
Whatever you call it,
whoever you are, you need one."

—Jane Howard

Families often provide us with a sense of belonging, security, and happiness. What does your support system or family look like? Draw each person you consider family and describe their importance to you.

Special connections are often present within the bigger family system. Is there someone in your immediate, extended, or chosen family to whom you are deeply connected? Describe them. What makes your connection special? What do you value about this connection?

Family conflict is inevitable; however, suffering from the conflict is optional. Is there someone in your family from whom you feel disconnected? What might be your reasons for the disconnection? What do you think their reasons might be?

If it serves you, in the postcard illustration below, practice reaching out to this person with the intention of reconnecting.

Connection often improves our physical and emotional well-being. Yet life can get busy, and staying connected to those we love can become more difficult. Name four important or significant members of your family. Then promise to make them a priority by writing a few enjoyable ways to stay connected to each.

RELATIONSHIPS

"THE BEST THING TO HOLD ONTO IN LIFE IS EACH OTHER."

—Audrey Hepburn

Identifying the ways that we express and feel love can help provide insight into our individual relationship needs. Some people show and feel love by spending time with their partner, buying sentimental gifts, or being physically close. What is your love language? How do you experience love? How do you show love?

Becoming aware of our needs in a romantic relationship can be helpful to ourselves and our partner. What are all the things you need in a relationship?

Learning from our past relationships can help inform our future relationships. Describe your dating history and/or significant romantic relationships you have had.

Looking at your history, what have you learned about yourself from those relationships? What have you noticed you are attracted to? How can you apply your learnings to your current or future relationships?

Expressing gratitude to a loved one can increase relationship satisfaction and longevity. Verbalizing your gratitude allows both of you to feel loved, heard, and seen. Let's practice on paper.

Thank you for...

I felt really grateful when you...

I noticed and felt so appreciative when you...

I am so thankful for your...

Now, let's express your gratitude directly. Close your journal for now and go tell your loved one how you feel. What was this experience like? What feelings came up after you expressed your gratitude?

COMMUNITY

"The greatness of a community is most accurately measured by the compassionate actions of its members."

—Coretta Scott King

Social connection is a necessity and part of the human experience. When we feel truly connected, we often experience a sense of unity, support, and joy. Who do you consider your people? Within the smallest circle, fill in the names of the people closest to you; for the second circle, fill in your friends and colleagues; and for the outer circle, fill in your acquaintances.

Look at your circles in the previous exercise. What kinds of feelings come to mind when you see the names of these people?

Pick one person from the previous exercise who brings up more positive feelings and explore your relationship with them. Then pick one person who brings up more negative feelings. Explore what those feelings may be about.

Giving back to our community can often make us feel connected and part of something bigger. Have you ever been part of something bigger within your community? Describe your experience. If not, what do you think it would it be like to engage in community service? Is there anything that holds you back?

Think about a time when you were kind to someone or engaged in an act of kindness. Describe the experience and how it made you feel.

Kindness is often contagious. Let's create a KAP (Kindness Activation Plan). During your week, either plan or list the act of kindness you did or plan to do, for whom, the date, and how it made you feel.

ACT OF KINDNESS:

FOR WHOM:

DATE:

ASSOCIATED FEELINGS:

ACT OF KINDNESS:

FOR WHOM:

DATE:

ASSOCIATED FEELINGS:

ACT OF KINDNESS:

FOR WHOM:

DATE:

ASSOCIATED FEELINGS:

CAREER & FINANCES

110

"DO WHAT YOU LOVE, AND SUCCESS WILL FOLLOW. PASSION IS THE FUEL BEHIND A SUCCESSFUL CAREER."

—Meg Whitman

Careers are a big piece of our life. Did you know the average person spends 90,000 hours at work over their entire lifetime? Yes, you read that correctly. Let's explore your career. Describe your current career path. What parts do you love? What parts do you wish you could change?

Landing or creating your dream career takes energy, effort, and positive thinking. At this moment, do you absolutely enjoy your career? If not, let's explore how to get you there. What does your dream career look like?

TYPE OF INDUSTRY:

SETTING:

PEOPLE:

CULTURE:

RESPONSIBILITIES:

TITLE:

SALARY:

HOURS:

What are three steps you can take today that get you a little closer to this dream career?

Money often has meaning attached to it. Meaning can stem from how we were raised, our current financial state, and our life dreams. When you think about money, what comes up? As a kid, what do you remember? How would you describe your relationship with money and its importance?

Let's imagine for a bit. If money did not exist, what would you be doing every day? What parts of your day would be the same, and what would you change? Would your career be different?

PASSIONS

"PASSION IS ENERGY. FEEL THE POWER THAT COMES FROM FOCUSING ON WHAT EXCITES YOU."

—Oprah Winfrey

Think back to when you were a child. What did you enjoy doing the most? What were your favorite activities? Describe and draw them.

Passion can be described as something that ignites pure joy, excitement, and enthusiasm within us. It is something that fills us up in ways that other things cannot. As an adult, what things excite you? What fills you up? Within each star, write what you feel passionately about. On the next page, elaborate on what each means to you.

We often think about our life in "if" statements. "If I had more money, I would . . . " or "If I didn't have to work, I would . . . " If you were given one day where money, time, and obligations were not a factor, what would you do? In what ways would your passions show up during your ideal day?

Passions can feel unachievable at times. We may have negative thoughts or assumptions about our ability to live out our true passions. What holds you back from your passions? What could you do to change these limitations?

For the upcoming week, how could you integrate some of your passions into each day?

GOALS & DREAMS

"YOU NEED TO GO FROM WANTING TO CHANGE YOUR LIFE TO DECIDING TO CHANGE YOUR LIFE. IF YOU WANT TO LIVE A LIFE YOU'VE NEVER LIVED, YOU HAVE TO DO THINGS YOU'VE NEVER DONE."

—Jen Sincero

Dreams help us define what we want out of life. What dreams do you have for yourself? When you think about your career, relationships, love, and possessions, what dreams come to mind? In the circles below, write your big and small dreams. On the next page, describe what each means to you.

Looking at the dreams you identified in the previous exercise, is there anything that prevents you from going after them? What fears come up? What do you find yourself afraid of?

Process goals and outcome goals provide a road map to your ultimate dream. An outcome goal is the ideal result (e.g., learning a second language). A process goal defines the skills you need to achieve the outcome (e.g., taking classes). Pick a few dreams from the first exercise and write out the specific skills needed for each to achieve the ultimate outcome.

According to a Dominican University of California study, you are 42 percent more likely to achieve your goals if you write them down. Let's get writing! What will you accomplish in the next few years?

In one year, I will...

In three years, I will...

In five years, I will...

The same study found that more than 70 percent of the participants who sent weekly updates to a friend about their goal progress reported successful goal achievement, compared to 35 percent of those who kept their goals to themselves. Who can you designate as your "goal friend"?

LIFE PURPOSE

"My mission in life is not merely to survive, but to thrive; and to do so with some passion, some compassion, some humor, and some style."

—Maya Angelou

When you read the word "purpose," what comes to mind? Without thinking much, jot down any words and phrases, and describe any images that pop into your mind.

Our life purpose is often rooted in our uniqueness as a person. In the diagram below, answer the questions in each circle. On the next page, write about any ideas that come to mind as you feel they relate to your overall life purpose.

WHAT ARE YOUR SKILLS
AND STRENGTHS?

WHAT DO YOU LOVE?
WHAT COMES EASY TO YOU?

WHAT ARE YOUR
CORE VALUES?

WHEN DO YOU FEEL LIKE
YOUR MOST AUTHENTIC SELF?

This world is a wonderful place because of the unique people who do great things in it. When we think of life purpose, we can also imagine how we want to leave our mark in this world or in our communities. What mark will you leave? What are the main things for which you would like to be remembered?

Based on how you would like to be remembered, create a detailed bucket list of the most important and emotionally fulfilling things—big and small—that you plan to accomplish in your lifetime.

REFLECTIONS

Wow, look at you! You committed to the journey of self-discovery and have come out on the other side—revealing the true you. Being brave enough to explore yourself on a deeper level takes tremendous courage. Sometimes it is so scary or foreign that we spend our entire life avoiding the parts of ourselves we feel unsure about. You did the very opposite. You should feel so proud for taking that step.

We are constantly evolving as humans, and when we grow with awareness, we can reach levels of true joy and contentment. It is important to know that self-discovery is a lifelong process. We are in a continual state of learning, growth, and fine-tuning. Life will continue to throw us different challenges, and through these challenges, we learn more about ourselves. I encourage you to keep digging and continue to have an open heart and mind.

Take some time to look back at your completed journal, now and in the future.

What was this experience like for you?

What were your favorite parts?

What did you find the most challenging?

What are three new things you learned about yourself?

Thank you for allowing me to guide you on your journey. If you ever question yourself or feel a sense of doubt, know that you often have all the answers within, and it usually just takes a bit of unwrapping to find them. I want to recognize you for your effort, intention, and strength to allow yourself the opportunity to grow in a way that will serve you endlessly. May you continue to cultivate and live as your authentic self while finding your optimal path in life.

"Always be a first-rate version of yourself, instead of a second-rate version of somebody else."

—Judy Garland

 RESOURCES

BOOKS

The Gifts of Imperfection: Let Go of Who You Think You're Supposed to Be and Embrace Who You Are by Brené Brown, 2010.

The Four Tendencies: The Indispensable Personality Profiles That Reveal How to Make Your Life Better (and Other People's Lives Better, Too) by Gretchen Rubin, 2017.

You Are a Badass: How to Stop Doubting Your Greatness and Start Living an Awesome Life by Jen Sincero, 2013.

Option B: Facing Adversity, Building Resilience, and Finding Joy by Sheryl Sandberg and Adam Grant, 2017.

REFERENCES

BrainyQuotes. "Audrey Hepburn Quotes." https://www.brainyquote.com/quotes/audrey_hepburn_378280.

BrainyQuotes. "Coretta Scott King Quotes." https://www.brainyquote.com/quotes/coretta_scott_king_810146.

BrainyQuotes. "Helen Keller Quotes." https://www.brainyquote.com/quotes/helen_keller_101301.

BrainyQuotes. "Judy Garland Quotes." https://www.brainyquote.com/quotes/judy_garland_104276.

BrainyQuotes. "Maya Angelou Quotes." https://www.brainyquote.com/quotes/maya_angelou_634520.

BrainyQuotes. "Oprah Winfrey Quotes." https://www.brainyquote.com/quotes/oprah_winfrey_384837.

Brown, Brené. *The Gifts of Imperfection: Let Go of Who You Think You're Supposed to Be and Embrace Who You Are.* Center City, MN: Hazelden Publishing, 2010.

Dominican University of California. "Study Focuses on Strategies for Achieving Goals, Resolutions." May 2015. https://www.dominican.edu/dominicannews/study-highlights-strategies-for-achieving-goals.

Goodreads. "C. JoyBell C. > Quotes > Quotable Quote." https://www.goodreads.com/quotes/449507-the-most-adventurous-journey-to-embark-on-is-the-journey.

Goodreads. "Marianne Williamson > Quotes > Quotable Quote." https://www.goodreads.com/quotes/964239-you-must-learn-a-new-way-to-think-before-you.

Harper's Bazaar. "My Cultural Life: Blake Lively." https://www.harpersbazaar.com/uk/culture/culture-news/news/a31402/my-cultural-life-blake-lively/.

Howard, Jane. *Families.* Piscataway, NJ: Transaction Publishers, 1999.

Ling, Kristi. *Operation Happiness: The 3-Step Plan to Creating a Life of Lasting Joy, Abundant Energy, and Radical Bliss.* New York, NY: Rodale Books, 2016.

Pryce-Jones, Jessica. *Happiness at Work: Maximizing Your Psychological Capital for Success.* West Sussex, UK: John Wiley & Sons, 2010.

Purcell, Maud. "The Health Benefits of Journaling." Psych Central. October 8, 2018. https://psychcentral.com/lib/the-health-benefits-of-journaling/.

QuoteFancy. "Meg Whitman Quotes." https://quotefancy.com/quote/1468353/Meg-Whitman-Do-what-you-love-and-success-will-follow-Passion-is-the-fuel-behind-a.

Sincero, Jen. *You Are a Badass: How to Stop Doubting Your Greatness and Start Living an Awesome Life.* Philadelphia, PA: Running Press Adult, 2013.

TreasureQuotes. "Sheila Murray Bethel Quotes." https://www.treasurequotes.com/quotes/one-of-the-most-courageous-things-you-can-do-i.

Walker, Lucy. "All Rise: Emma Watson on female power, facing her fears, and love without rules." *Porter Magazine*, Winter Escape, 2015.

The White House, President Barack Obama. "Remarks by the First Lady at Tuskegee University Commencement Address." May 9, 2015. https://obamawhitehouse.archives.gov/the-press-office/2015/05/09/remarks-first-lady-tuskegee-university-commencement-address.

ACKNOWLEDGMENTS

I feel endless gratitude for my people: my husband, son, mom, sister, and best friend. You have played such a pivotal role in making all my dreams come true. Thank you for your unconditional love and support. Thank you to Callisto Media for providing me the opportunity to write about a topic I feel so passionately about. Our individual potential is limitless when we begin to open our eyes to ourselves.

ABOUT THE AUTHOR

Dr. Kelly Vincent is a licensed psychologist (PSY30672) and registered yoga teacher working in private practice in Encinitas, California. She obtained her master's and doctoral degrees in clinical psychology. Her areas of specialty include working with women, young adults, moms, and female entrepreneurs. She uses an integrative mind-body approach in therapy, as she feels passionately about treating clients holistically. Dr. Vincent is also the co-founder of Movement Therapy Spaces, a coworking-inspired office space for therapists and holistic providers located in North County, San Diego. She is devoted to mental health advocacy and reducing the stigma of going to therapy. She explores such topics on her professional Instagram account (@dr.kellyvincent). She resides in Cardiff-by-the-Sea, California, with her husband, son, and goldendoodle.

ABOUT THE ILLUSTRATOR

Jacinta Kay is is a hand letterer and illustrator from Melbourne, Australia. She is inspired by the magical, the mystical, and all things natural and ephemeral. Her work aims to combine fun letterforms with delicate patterns that continue to surprise and delight long after the first viewing. When she's not creating letterforms, drawing flowers, or writing long, emotional captions for Instagram, she's trying to help others find the same happiness and purpose that she's found in pursuing creativity and goal fulfillment.

CPSIA information can be obtained
at www.ICGtesting.com
Printed in the USA
JSHW012259221020
8710JS00001B/1

9 781646 116331